South Africa
For Kids
People, Places and Cultures
Children Explore The World Books

SPEEDY
PUBLISHING

Speedy Publishing LLC
40 E. Main St. #1156
Newark, DE 19711
www.speedypublishing.com

Copyright 2015

Let's learn some interesting facts about South Africa!

The official name
of South Africa
is the Republic
of South Africa.

In 2011 the population of South Africa was around 52 million.

South Africa has three capital cities, Cape Town, Bloemfontein and Pretoria.

South Africa has 11 official languages, including Zulu, Afrikaans, Xhosa and English.

South Africa
has the largest
economy of any
African country.

Nelson Mandela was elected president in 1994 after South Africa's first universal elections.

South Africa's coastline stretches over 2500 kilometres (1553 miles) in length.

South Africa is home to a wide variety of animals including giraffes, hippopotamus, leopards and lions.

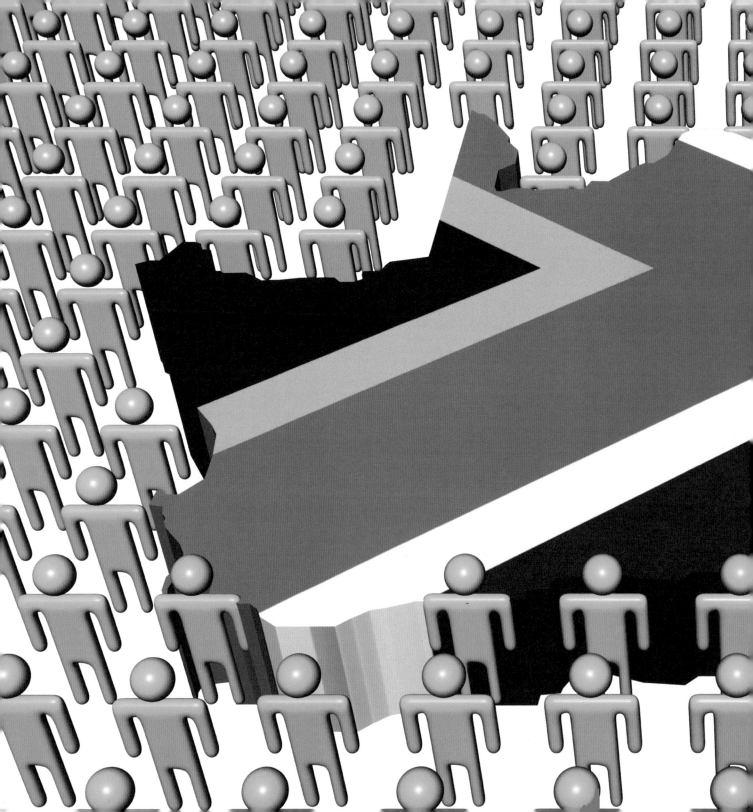

South Africa
has high
unemployment.

The first
human heart
transplant was
performed
in a Cape
Town hospital
in 1967.

Cave paintings have been found in South Africa that date to around 75000 years ago.

South Africa's drinking water is rated 3rd best in the world for being "safe and ready to drink".

South Africa is the only country in the entire world that has voluntarily abandoned its nuclear weapons programme.

South Africa is home to the oldest meteor scar in the world – the Vredefort Dome in a town called Parys. The site is a UNESCO World Heritage Site.

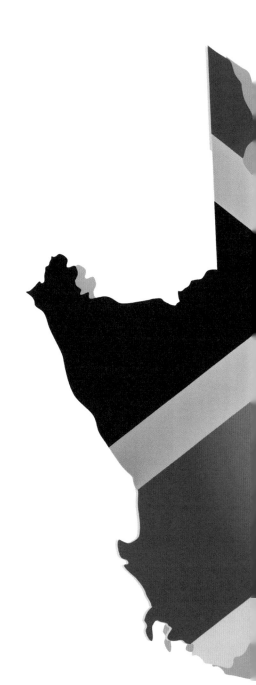

South Africa
is home to
the highest
commercial
bungi jump
in the world
at 710 feet.

The South African Rovos Rail is considered the most luxurious train in the world.

The oldest remains
of modern humans
were found in
South Africa and
are well over
160,000 years old.

South Africa has a lot to offer and you should visit the country soon and explore!

Printed in Great Britain
by Amazon